I0073834

RYT

ROMANCE YOUR TRIBE™
ONLINE

CLIENT ATTRACTION IN ACTION

**52 ACTION PACKED *CUSTOMER ATTRACTING IDEAS*
...AND MORE!**

JANET BECKERS
AND FRIENDS

About The Author

Australian Janet Beckers is a sought after international speaker, best-selling author and multi-award winning entrepreneur including Australian Marketer of The Year.

Janet specialises in helping authors, coaches, speakers and small business owners step up, step out and get their message out to the world with her signature RYT training programs.

She lives on the Central Coast of NSW Australia, adores her husband and 2 teenage children, is a passionate life-saver and runner and one day will learn to stand up on her surf board.

Other Publications by the Author

Romance Your Tribe Online: *The Five (and a half) Steps To Create a Tribe of Loyal Fans Who LOVE Your Brand.*

The Power of 100: *100 International Women Share Powerful Stories of How to Stay Focused on Your Dreams*

Our Internet Secrets: *How to Find Financial Freedom on the Internet*

Training Programs by the Author

RYT: 90 Day Program

Shine Online Coaching

MeTV Program

Wonderful Web Women

Wonderful Web Inner Circle

Romance Your Tribe Online

Client Attraction in Action

52 Action Packed Customer Attracting Ideas…..and MORE!

By

Janet Beckers

Published by Wonderful Web Press
Australia

Romance Your Tribe Online:
Client Attraction in Action

First published in Australia by
Wonderful Web Press,
a division of Niche Partners Pty Ltd

PO Box 6356
Kincumber. NSW 2251
Australia

Copyright © 2015 Janet Beckers

www.RomanceYourTribe.com

All rights reserved. No part of this publication may be reproduced or transmitted by any means electronic, photocopying or otherwise without the prior written permission of the author.

National Library of Australia Cataloguing-in-Publication entry:

Author: Janet Beckers

Title: Romance Your Tribe Online: *Client Attraction in Action*

ISBN: 978-0-9870944-2-1

Subjects: Business, Internet.

To Phoebe and Clancy Beckers
Phoebe the Queen of Lists and Natural
Connector, and
Clancy the Born Entrepreneur.
I Love watching you both grow and watch in
awe as you make your stamp on the world.

Contents

	Chapter	Page #
I.	List of Contributors	8
II.	Acknowledgements	9
1.	Not Your Typical Team	10
2.	How To Make The Most of This Book	12
3.	Romance, Tribes and Action	14
4.	Flirting	17
5.	Back to My Place	35
6.	Courting	47
7.	Romance	67
8.	Commitment	81
9.	Bonus Chapter	97

List of Contributors

- Ayesha Hilton
- Belinda Bowler
- Belinda Jackson
- Carol Davies
- Cate Richards
- Cheryl Ueding
- Clancy Lee Beck
- Cynde Canepa
- Elliot Violette
- Emily Miller
- Gail Bennell
- Judith Briggs
- Karen Thomson
- Kathleen Gage
- Kathryn Kitto
- Kay Ross
- Kerrie Phipps
- Lauren Mescon
- Linda Claire Puig
- Lisa McAdams
- Lisa McDonald
- Lisa Tassell
- Louise Bedford
- Louise Brogan
- Luanne Simmons
- Monika Mundell
- Nancy A. Barnes
- Paul Godden
- Paula Tarrant
- Samantha Hartley
- Urszula Richards

Acknowledgements

Thank you to my fellow contributing authors. This opportunity was offered to thousands of people and you are the ones who stepped up and took action. You inspire me. Thanks also to the many beautiful people in my online community who gave feedback throughout the process on things as varied as helping me choose the title, the cover graphics, the promotional blurbs and contributed marketing ideas. This truly is a collaborative book.

A HUGE thank you to my wonderful assistant Ferraiza Velasquez who stepped up to learn new skills with enthusiasm and kept everything running smoothly.

A huge thank you to my beautiful family Douglas, Phoebe and Clancy Beckers who always back me in everything I do and envelope me in love and laughter. 16 year old Clancy suggested the title "Client Attraction in Action".

Big thanks to my mum Beverly Wood because, well, she's my mum!

And last but not least, a huge thanks to you beautiful reader. You wouldn't be reading this book if you didn't have a dream. It is the entrepreneurs with a dream that truly motivate me to create opportunities for you to take action. If you'd like to join us as a contributor in our next book, I'd love to invite you to join our community so we can shine the light on you too.

Not Your Typical Team

This book is the result of team work – but not your typical team!

The team who created this publication are spread throughout the globe. Contributors come from all parts of the world ... from Australia to the USA, from Canada to France, from New Zealand to Great Britain.

Every part of this book, from concept to title, every article, artwork, formatting, distribution and marketing – everything – has been the result of the collaboration of members of the Wonderful Web Tribe. Each contributor is a business partner or an Inner Circle member of the Wonderful Web Women community who not only saw an opportunity, BUT TOOK ACTION.

Action is what has set the authors and contributors of this book apart from everyone else and that is why action is the purpose of this book.

Focus on Action
Each idea is designed with action in mind

Each author's ideas and tips are as varied as the businesses they operate and the countries where they work and live. Each tip has this is common: they have all been tested and work in the authors' own businesses and will work for you too. Here are just a few of the things you'll learn:

- Clever ways to use Facebook to build customer loyalty
- Video tips to make your viewer feel you are talking to them personally
- Creative ways to surprise your customers and make them say "wow"
- How to keep your clients talking about your events months after they go home
- Clever ways to make your website a client magnet and makes them think "this is where I belong"
- Thoughtful ways to connect via email, phone and in person

Plus more. With over 52 simple and actionable ideas, I encourage you to commit to focusing on just one tip each week and take action to implement it in your business. Do this, and you'll see exponential growth in your business this year and you will inspire deeper loyalty from your clients.

For Businesses Who Care

This book has been created for business people, coaches, authors, speakers and service providers who know the true gold in their business comes from the loyalty of their customers, and want simple, and powerful ideas to consistently attract perfect clients. You know, the type of clients who pay without complaining, value your services and become loyal fans who LOVE your brand.

Flick through the book, choose a page at random and unearth a simple and tested idea you can do THIS WEEK to attract your perfect customer to you.

Gift for You

I have a gift to help you build a strong business and brand that gets your message out to the world....in a meaningful and profitable way.

Online Tribal Business Leader Quick Start Kit

Get crystal clear on the steps you need to take, in the RIGHT ORDER, to quickly build your lifestyle business and position yourself as a Tribal Business Leader Online. Includes video, eBook, audio training and powerful one-page action checklists personalised for each of the 4 entrepreneur types.

This training is free and no credit card is needed. Access it here:

www.RomanceYourTribe.com/actiongift

How to Make the Most of This Book

This book is about ideas and making incremental changes to the way you do business that combine to make your brand irresistible to your ideal customer.

I recommend you use this book in one of the following ways:

One per Week Method

If you really want to see big changes in the attractiveness of your brand, then planned and systematic action will get you there every time. There are more than 52 tried and tested strategies in this book so I challenge you to systematically implement one idea to your business, every week for the next year.

How do I know this works? Because I've done it.

When I started my business Wonderful Web Women, I had a young business and a steep learning curve ahead of me. As part of my business model, I interviewed a different successful woman every week for over 2 years. I made a commitment to myself to implement just 1 strategy I learnt from every speaker every single week. I didn't try and do everything. I chose one simple and do-able strategy and applied it without fail every single week.

Within a year my business had grown so much, and my tribe was so loyal to me and my brand, that I had already won numerous awards, been invited internationally to be an event speaker and my profitability had sky-rocketed.

So committed, incremental improvement works.

Get Unstuck Method

This is a great way to use this book.

Are you stuck for ideas on how to get new leads? Maybe you need to increase how much each customer spends with you or you feel the need to energise your email campaigns or website?

Flick through the book, choose a page at random and unearth a simple and tested idea you can do THIS WEEK to attract your perfect customer to you.

I Know It All Method

Well, this is not really the method I recommend you use but I know there will be a portion of readers who adopt this method.

You see, the thing with effective marketing, is it is usually the established methods that work best. So as you flick through the book you may think to yourself "I know that, I've thought of that" etc.

But my question to you is *Have you implemented?*

Don't discount an idea because it is not radically cutting edge. Instead, acknowledge the difference between knowledge and results and commit to use one of the methods above.

Romance, Tribes and Action

The process of finding potential new clients and moving through the process of becoming a paying customer, in fact a raving fan, is very much like a romance. If you try to go for the hard sell too quick, you'll leave them feeling like a one-night-stand! If you treat every new lead in your business as if they are going to be "The One' you will spend the rest of your (business) life with, then you will see how the Romance Your Tribe model works to build a business of customers committed to you for life!

Bonus Chapter "Tribes and Romance"

To dive in and really understand how tribes online work, at the end of the book, I've included a bonus chapter from the Amazon #1 Best Selling book *"Romance Your Tribe Online: The 5 (and a half) Steps To Create A Tribe Of Loyal Fans That Love Your Brand"*.

You may even want to flick to the bonus chapter first so you can get a deeper understanding of how you can strategically use the ideas shared by our contributing authors.

The 5 Steps to Romance Your Tribe

The ideas in this book are structured around the steps in the "Romance Your Tribe" trademarked system. The bonus chapter will give you more detail but I'll introduce you to each step below.

As you'll see, the model allows me to have a bit of fun when teaching about business. An opportunity to talk about push-up bras and getting lucky. But don't let the frivolity fool you. This is a system that build a very strong foundation to create a tribe of loyal fans who love YOUR brand.

I've attempted to sort the ideas shared by our authors into one of the 5 categories so, if you are looking for ways to increase customer retention, for example, you can flick to the section called "Commitment". As you'll see though, many of the tips can easily fit into more than one category so feel free to mix and match to your needs.

The 5 steps to create your Tribal Platform are:

- ✓ Flirting
- ✓ Back to My Place
- ✓ Courting
- ✓ Romance
- ✓ Commitment

Flirting

Flirting is the stage most people think about when it comes to marketing your business online. This is the traffic generation part. The part of the business building cycle where you put on your sexiest clothes, paint on the lippy, put on the push-up bra, scan the headlines so you'll have something to talk about and head out to find your soul mate (men, you can skip the lippy and push-up bra OK). The business building equivalent is finding great sources of your ideal customer and making such a great impression on them they can't wait to get back to your place.

In this section, we share some ideas to help you find and attract new leads to your business who are most likely to spend money with you and consistently bring new traffic to your website.

Back to My Place

Now you've been out flirting around you should have lots and lots of gorgeous potential customers excited to get to know you better. It's time to invite them back to your place. Like in a romance, you want to make sure, when you invite them home, that the place is looking the best it can. In romance, this would mean cleaning up, strategically placing your trophy collection somewhere they will notice, putting on some mood music, candles and generally making them feel so comfortable and welcome they agree to a second date.

In business (and list building specifically), this means ensuring your web site is designed to convert visitors you attract to become subscribers on your list.

In this section you've attracted your ideal client, now let's look at some tips so your website and place of business is designed to convert visitors you attract to become subscribers on your list. We want them to know they have found "Home" when they find you.

15 **Janet Beckers**

Courting

The courting phase is where you're really keeping in touch with them. They're ready for another date with you, and you're serious about developing a lasting relationship with them. In online terms, after they've signed up for your e-mail list, you'll follow up with your newsletter and your e-mail auto-responders.

Hey, you may have made it to the second date and your perfect client has joined your mailing list, but, just as in a romance, don't assume they are a sure thing. At this stage the relationship is still a bit one-sided. You are still doing the hard work to impress.

In this section, there's some ideas to sweep them off their feet with your communication before you start making the sale.

Romance

This is where they're starting to give you a little attention now – they're starting to get "into" you. If you've swept your client off their feet by courting them then they will now be "into" you. The relationship is going both ways and that's what you want to encourage.

Here's some ideas to give you strategies to encourage your clients to interact with you and your brand.

Commitment

This is where you're looking forward to a long-term relationship – and in romantic terms, this would be where you might start thinking about children. In business, this is where they become your customer, where they purchase your products – a very big step! They may start with your less-expensive products – a perfectly reasonable way to start! – and they'll go on to become a loyal customer who'll spend more and more money over time... and become a devoted, dedicated fan.

In this section we share some ideas to help you wow your customer after the sale and keep them loyal to you forever.

Flirting

Here's some ideas to help you find and attract new leads to your business who are most likely to spend money with you and consistently bring new traffic to your website.

Remember our Gift to you:
Online Tribal Business Leader Quick Start Kit

www.RomanceYourTribe.com/actiongift

Love in a Tube

If a picture paints a thousand words, a video will <u>flood</u> your customer with Love.

So here's how to share that Love with over a billion visitors to YouTube every day.

1. Identify your 'ideal' customer and plan the messages you want to convey to them (eg testimonial, product/service review, competition, about me/us)
2. Always end videos with a Call To Action (like, share, buy)
3. Use a smartphone or video camera to record your videos (keep them under 3 minutes)
4. Create your channel on YouTube and upload videos
5. Title your video(s) with terms people search for (eg 'How To Apply Lipstick' not 'Acme Lipstick') but include your keyword (lipstick)
6. Put in Tags all the relevant keywords (eg lipstick, put on lipstick, apply lipstick etc)
7. Put as much detail as possible in Description box starting with your website url including the 'http://' and have your keyword appear twice in description
8. Share the video link with your customers as well as on social media and your website and blog

So go grab some TLC (Tube Liking Customers) as well as boost your website SEO with some Love sucking videos on YouTube.

About the Author: Paul Godden

Paul Godden brings over 30 years working with video to a range of programs showing anybody how to tap into and use the power of video. Programs include 'Video Made Easy for Business', 'iVideo Mastery', 'Tube Video Domination', 'Animated Biz Videos' and other programs.

Connect with the Author

www.RomanceYourTribe.com/paulgodden

Romance Your Customers: treat every new lead in your business as if they are going to be "The One" you will spend the rest of your (business) life with

Book Quotes with Janet Beckers
www.RomanceYourTribe.com

The Power of Noticing and Being Noticed

A lot of social media is about noticing and being noticed. It feels good when you are positively noticed for something you did or said, doesn't it? Well, it feels good to other people too. Most people have a deep need to be seen and heard. Relationships begin with noticing and build from there. Here are some tips you can do even if you only have 10 minutes a day!

On Facebook, send your client a message, ask to be their friend, comment on something they said or commented on, 'like' something they said or commented on. Visit groups and pages related to your business and see if you can engage by answering questions or sharing useful information.

On Twitter, send a tweet to mention your client, reply to one of their tweets or 'retweet' what they said. Follow a topic that they are 'tweeting' about for research on client attraction.

On LinkedIn, build your connections by adding 5 new people, post an update on a group your clients are following, ask or answer a question there or contact your client directly.

Be the person who notices your client to attract their business.

About the Author: Emily Miller

Emily Miller is a tech savvy, heart-centered Virtual Assistant and Online Media Goddess. Her clients are Rising Stars ready for the next level of success and visibility. She provides high vibration done for you services, removing your overwhelm, to create a conscious consistent online presence that delivers a profitable return.

Connect with the Author

www.RomanceYourTribe.com/emilymiller

Facebook, Twitter And Linked In, Oh My!

Be short and to the point to get that very short attention span of the social media surfer, about 9 seconds.

Start with twitter. When you have a flash or brilliance, put your thought out to the universe. Find people who are brilliant and retweet or favorite what they say, and it will go to your followers.

Facebook pages are perfect to daily intersperse posts about your product if you are selling, or your business, if you have an opportunity. Use your page to show your gratitude for your business, to highlight a customer or a business partner and say how proud you are of them. Use your page to offer a weekly tip in your area of expertise. For example, on Tuesdays, I show a transformation of a customer, as a result of using our skin care products. On Saturdays, I have Success Story Saturday and share a success story of a business partner. Choose either a theme or a weekly post and be consistent with it.

Linked in is excellent for connecting with like-minded professional people. Form your own linked in group or join a small one and engage.

About the Author: Lauren Mescon

Lauren Gordon Mescon, attorney and former family court judge, was introduced to the entrepreneurial world of Rodan + Fields and direct sales by a lifelong friend. She was immediately hooked and today has a successful business which she can work from anywhere with only a laptop and nearby coffee shop!

Connect with the Author

www.RomanceYourTribe.com/laurenmescon

If you are ready to step up and to be the leader in your tribe, the excuse that 'I'm not good enough' or 'I'm not quite ready yet' is something that you are going to have to give up

Book Quotes with Janet Beckers
www.RomanceYourTribe.com

There's Power in the Name

Names are incredibly powerful things. Including your name _____ ! (insert yours here) ☺

Names are identifiers, open doors and create connections. How do you feel when you walk into a café or store and you're greeted enthusiastically – by name? When you have those encounters with someone who may not remember you and they call out your name with a smile on their face? Your sense of status and connectedness increases and the happy chemicals burst from your brain throughout your whole system and even your posture improves. So how can you increase the connection with your customers?

Ask their name – be willing to offer yours first. Use it in conversation. If you're on the phone, write it down. Be honest if it's slipped your mind. They'll appreciate that it matters to you. Bluffing your way can be more obvious than you think. Use their name to introduce them to others. This places value on them and improves the relationship. Use this approach with EVERYONE. Each person you meet has a name and a story and a life that matters.

Dale Carnegie "Names are the sweetest and most important sound in any language."

About the Author: Kerrie Phipps

Passionate about education and inspiring social change, Kerrie Phipps is a professional speaker, author and leadership coach for world-changers.

Her most recent book Do Talk to Strangers – How to Connect with Anyone, Anywhere, is inspiring extraordinary conversations globally, as Kerrie and her audience live the message of Connecting with Confidence.

Connect with the Author

www.RomanceYourTribe.com/kerriephipps

Business Development. Personal Development. Same Thing.

Book Quotes *with Janet Beckers*
www.RomanceYourTribe.com

Conscious Social Media

One thing I advise my clients to keep in mind when using social media is to be 'conscious'. Choose to put your heart and soul in it. Be yourself. Speak your truth. And use social media to practice conscious communication.

A whole lot of posts about what you ate for breakfast this morning are probably not going to attract a lot of interested people to your Profile. And they might turn some people off (unless nutrition is your business).

To give your posts extra depth and power, take a moment to be still inside yourself *before* you share anything on **Facebook, Twitter or LinkedIn**.

Check in with your heart, and imagine the hearts of the people that you are wanting to reach most.

What might they most need to hear or see right now? A bit of humour, or some action steps, an inspiring quote... Let your intuition guide you.

If you can take a moment to drop into your heart before you post on Facebook, LinkedIN or Twitter, you are much more likely to write something that will resonate deeply in other people's hearts. And in this way, you can grow the great work that you do.

About the Author: Emily Miller

Emily Miller is a tech savvy, heart-centered Virtual Assistant and Online Media Goddess. Her clients are Rising Stars ready for the next level of success and visibility. She provides high vibration done for you services, removing your overwhelm, to create a conscious consistent online presence that delivers a profitable return.

Connect with the Author

www.RomanceYourTribe.com/emilymiller

Being Generous Gets Noticed

I've discovered being generous gets noticed. My tip to form relationships is to play an active role in forums where entrepreneurs hang out.

I initially "lurked" in forums, believing I had little to teach successful people. One day I noticed a post which proposed a clanger of a branding mistake. Here were a lot of "natural" marketers, who had built brands on gut instinct - yet they were asking great questions and looking for support.

With my corporate marketing background finally put to some use, I started answering posts. I would include my reasoning and some teaching notes. Response was great, both public acknowledgement and private messages. I even have VIP clients from these groups.

Whilst perceived to be giving, I receive far more in the form of insight. I fully understand the struggle with clarity. I know the places people get stuck or go wrong strategically. I've learned to structure my teaching content for simplicity and useability.

Look around for your ideal milieu. Paid forums can be better because there are more committed people, though there are some good private groups as well. Ask around where friends get value, like me, you may just get far more than you give.

About the Author: Cate Richards
Cate Richards of True Entrepreneur: If your business hasn't taken flight, you may have a clarity problem. Clarity must come before marketing activity. Operating from your sweet spot, where you access your true ability, allows other activity to flow. I guide entrepreneurs to unearth their foundation and then I watch them build their dreams.

Connect with the Author
www.RomanceYourTribe.com/caterichards

Share The Love Via A Blogs & Social Media

A great way to show appreciation for your customers is to promote them on social media, on your website or blog, or as a case study in your marketing. If your customer has a win, why not share their success!

In my work with entrepreneurs, coaches and business owners, I happily promote them on my Facebook and Twitter accounts. It exposes them to a wider audience as well and they love it.

Don't forget to like your customers' Facebook pages and follow them on Twitter. Engage with their content and share if appropriate. The more followers and fans they have and the more engagement they have on their social media the better.

If you have a blog, you could invite your customers to write a guest post to help them reach a new audience. Alternatively, if your customers have a blog, you could write a guest post for them. This shows your love and appreciation and gives them some great content to share with their readers, as well as helping your visibility.

Another great way to promote customers is by featuring them in a case study that you share with your followers, fans, and email subscribers.

About the Author: Ayesha Hilton

Ayesha Hilton is an author, speaker, and business strategist. She helps business owners, consultants, coaches and entrepreneurs grow their business and brand by becoming a published author. She is passionate about helping people do what they love while earning a great income.

Connect With the Author

www.RomanceYourTribe.com/ayeshahilton

Using Social Media To Find Your Tribe

In today's online world, social media (SM) is used for a variety of business applications, including finding your tribe and inviting them to join you. Most people log onto to SM on a daily basis. Use SM to find your ideal client on Blogs, Google+, Facebook, LinkedIn, Twitter, YouTube, Pinterest, Instagram etc. Here are some basic ideas to get your own SM campaign started;

1. Set up a branded page on each SM site, including your own blog
2. Post on other people's blogs and SM sites. Add to their discussions and become known an expert in your field
3. Brainstorm a list of topics and develop them ahead of time
4. Decide on an incentive (gift) to encourage people to sign up – after all, you want their contact details in return for giving them something of value
5. Post regularly; these must all reflect the 'brand' that you are promoting
6. Respond daily to posts and comments Using SM to find your ideal client and invite them on board makes good business sense. After all, we all know that we need to get to know someone first before we commit!

About The Author: Kay Ross

Kay's expertise in health, education, coaching and online business growth is the basis for her success. She developed "Nurse Wellness Project" and "Nurse Biz Solutions" to support nurse's health and wellness and business development. Kay used social media to reach over 6000 nurses to talk about their health and wellness.

Connect With the Author

www.RomanceYourTribe.com/kayross

Give Customers Great Deals on Facebook

Give the right attention to your customers. Are you using Facebook for unique customer service? Accent Marketing's 2014 survey "Customer Engagement and Today's Consumer" shows 82% of companies use and trust Facebook for information on products and services.

Its 2014 Survey "Customer Engagement and Today's Consumer" found two thirds of consumers use Facebook to find good deals and promotions, including 80 percent of Baby Boomers. What a great alternative channel to prospect repeat business from customers or gain new ones.

As part of your customer service, always obtain the Facebook account information from your clients and get permission to add them to your list. Have a well-defined target market information strategy for your customers. Regularly send this list special promotions or information about new services geared to their business interests. Post the same information on your business Facebook fan page.

Ask customers for feedback on a new product or service. Consumers like to engage in dialogue with a company or endorse a great new product. Use Facebook as part of your marketing strategy. It's an easy way to be proactive with your customers, get their views on your products or new orders too.

About the Author: Carol Davies

Carol Davies is a certified success coach, speaker and author with Passion Motivator Coaching. She helps busy women and entrepreneurs who are overwhelmed in personal and/or business life find their passion, get focused, devise a life plan and achieve success with joy and ease.

Connect with the Author

www.RomanceYourTribe.com/caroldavies

Wow This Could Be My Next Blog!

In order to gain a connection and trust, I like to connect with my potential clients about what interests them. One of the ways I do this is once we've connected on Facebook, I will follow their posts or I get my PA to follow them for me. I will like their positive posts, so they start to think of me as part of their world. This builds trust and familiarity and is also a good way to gauge if we would be a good fit working together.

When they post something that relates to fear or, more importantly, fear holding them back, I will comment on the post from the position of expert and offer some information or advice I know will help them. I say that I find this is common with my clients and that I would like to write a blog about it. But out of respect I wanted to ask if they were okay with that and, unless they want me to, I promise not to mention their name. This lets them know they can trust me. I ask them to send me a Personal Message, if they prefer. We now have a connection and I have separated myself from the crowd.

About the Author: Lisa McAdams
Lisa McAdams is an author, presenter and coach, who has been there and learned to embrace life after divorce and now lives every day by design not by default. Lisa specializes in showing other women how to create a happy, fulfilling, powerful life after divorce through her program Money, Men and Me.

Connect with the Author
www.RomanceYourTribe.com/lisamcadams

Build a vibrant, engaged community on Twitter

Twitter may have a reputation for mindless social chitter, but beneath the surface, twitter is home to multitudes vibrant communities that span the globe. You can harness the power of twitter and build your own vibrant community too.

As a Speech Pathologist, I've used twitter to build my own Professional Learning Network (PLN) to connect with health professionals across the globe. Not only do I learn from my colleagues, I share my expertise on communication, working with people with disabilities and growing a thriving, sustainable private practice too.

Here's how you can build your own Professional Learning Network:

1. Got a burning question? Ask it on twitter! You may be surprised at the conversations that follow.

2. Heading to a conference or seminar? Share the take home messages with your tribe, and build your reputation in your area of expertise. BONUS TIP: find event participants on Twitter before you go, and meet up in person when you arrive.

3. See someone else tweet something you agree with? Retweet it and let them, and your followers know about it.

About the Author: Gail Bennell
Gail is a Speech Pathologist who coaches parents of children with disabilities on Skype, so their kids can learn to communicate and reach their full potential. She also helps health professionals thriving build thriving private practices so they too can help their clients reach their full potential.

Connect with the Author
www.RomanceYourTribe.com/gailbennell

Do Talk To Strangers – They might become your best customers!

My parents, living and working on the family farm, have a global network of friends, without social media, without any internet. They talk to strangers. Travellers on the road, sometimes needing help with a flat tyre, sometimes fellow travellers they meet as they participate in skydive meets around the world. They talk to anyone, anywhere - they connect and extraordinary doors open. Their habits have rubbed off & this is how I've built an international business – by CONNECTING.

People I've met in shops and airports have paid me hundreds or thousands of dollars for coaching or speaking engagements. You just don't know who you're standing next to. Reach out. In curiosity, kindness and compassion. There's a big difference between seeing people as potential customers and seeing them as human beings like ourselves who have things on their minds, interesting stories to share, pains and joys. Be yourself and be open.

Want to grow a business or community group? Do Talk to Strangers - your world will never be the same, but larger, more colourful and thriving.

It's the people in your world who make up your world. Keep growing it!

About the Author: Kerrie Phipps
Kerrie Phipps is an engaging speaker and unique facilitator of strategic and inspiring connections across fields such as education, thought-leadership and entrepreneurship. Author of Do Talk to Strangers – How to Connect with Anyone, Anywhere, and Lifting The Lid on Quiet Achievers, Kerrie is passionate about connecting and empowering Leaders/Difference-Makers.

Connect with the Author
www.RomanceYourTribe.com/kerriephipps

Attract New Customers with Your Local Paper

Write articles for your local newspaper. Use the "special" pages where they have community focus that matches what you have to offer. In my case, I have written for the "Positive Ageing" section or the "Health/Wellness" section of our local free newspaper.

This gives a lot of people a look at you in a short space of time. If you do it repeatedly they get to "know" you, they get to see where you are coming from and they either like it or don't. Either way is good because when you write on subjects that you are aligned with and which are close to your heart you will naturally attract your target market and push away those who would waste your time.

This action has led to many people coming out to visit my shop and café – it has led them "back to my place". The people who have made the effort to visit are best suited to you - they have already demonstrated that by showing up.

The newspaper articles can be linked back to your website or Facebook. You could rewrite them as articles on your blog or, in my case, webTV.

About the Author: Cheryl Ueding

Cheryl Ueding (Australia) is the Owner and Founder of Soul Star Connections® and Producer of SoulStarConnectionswebTV… Shifting Gears in Your Life. She has developed spiritual self-development programs and home study courses: Shifting Gears®, Living Authentically, Be Your Own Healer… Be Your Own Life Coach; the Emotional Rescue® healing process and Facilitator Training of these. Co-author of Embraced by the Divine book.

Connect with the Author

www.RomanceYourTribe.com/cherylueding

Back To My Place

You've attracted your ideal client, now let's look at some tips so your website and place of business is designed to convert visitors you attract to become subscribers on your list. We want them to know they have found "Home" when they find you.

Remember our Gift to you:

Online Tribal Business Leader Quick Start Kit

www.RomanceYourTribe.com/actiongift

Commit or Run?

Most people run in the opposite direction when their brand new date ask them to "commit" to the relationship. It's the same with your online customers; if they've only just "met" you then don't immediately start asking them to move in!

I've had some online companies ask me to buy their product or sign up to their program when I've only just met them and don't even know who they are. Why would I commit my money, time and energy to someone I don't know?

So ... the bottom line is; develop a relationship BEFORE you ask for commitment. Provide quality content and the opportunity for your customers to see who you are. Respond to comments and answer questions, show up in your online groups and forums, blog regularly, offer advice and develop a relationship with your tribe.

You are more likely to continue to stay if you like someone and want to get to know them better. Treat your customers the same way and you'll find that they are more likely to "commit" because they know you and are ready to take the relationship further! Commitment doesn't have to be scary – make it fun and enjoy yourself!

About The Author: Kay Ross
Kay's expertise in health, education, coaching and online business growth is the basis for her success. She developed "Nurse Wellness Project" and "Nurse Biz Solutions" to support nurse's health and wellness and business development. Kay used social media to reach over 6000 nurses to talk about their health and wellness.

Connect With the Author
www.RomanceYourTribe.com/kayross

Every small action is a step forward and it is surprising how soon those small, consistent steps get you to the top of your mountain.

Book Quotes *with Janet Beckers*
www.RomanceYourTribe.com

Be a Client Attractor

The way to catch flies is not to chase them one by one, but to sit with a plate of food. They will soon come to you. How can you be that plate of food to potential customers? Be a client attractor, not a client chaser.

1. Be Black or White, but not grey. Nobody is inspired by wishy washy. You may repel a batch of people, but they were not your ideal clients anyway. Be awesome to fewer people, not average to many.

2. Focus on serving, not selling, and give enormous value. Potential customers will regard you as the trusted adviser rather than someone trying to get a client.

3. Have a step-by-step process or system to offer. It shows you have experience with a tried and tested method, and structure gives clients confidence that their outcome will be achieved.

4. Have clarity and confidence about your service, and declare it. Someone passionate about what they do is way more attractive than someone needy or desperate.

5. Have fun! Nothing is more attractive than someone having a good time.

Most of my personal training clients have come from focussing on the above points - and doing what I love and expressing it.

About the Author: Clancy Lee Beck

Clancy Lee Beck is the go-to personal trainer and weight loss coach for the over 40's who want to be Fit, Fabulous and Frisky.

From dynamic classes, to private strategy sessions and online courses, she helps clients achieve their lifestyle and body transformation goals.

Connect with the Author

www.RomanceYourTribe.com/clancyleebeck

Your Website Needs a Love Letter!

Love. Sweet. Love. The world needs more love. Even on our websites. It's time to add LOVE for greater connection.

In my work as a marketing strategist I know the marketing 'rules'. I know what's expected of a website. And I believe the time has come for something new. The time has come for more heart to heart connection online. It's time to drop the website 'rules' and cut through the clutter by being yourself and expressing from the heart to your ideal clients.

When someone turns up at your website greet them with a Love Letter. How you do this is simple - simply speak or write from your heart. Imagine arriving at a website and feeling it's meant for you, it speak to your desires and to what you're struggling with? Also, when we feel like someone loves what they do and wants to serve us it feels GOOD! We want more.

So quit what you think your page should 'say' and step into your heart. What's the message you want to express to your ideal prospective customer who has just landed on your page? How can you make them feel welcome, like they've arrived in the right place, and wanting more...

About the Author: Belinda Jackson
As an Online Business & Marketing Strategist Belinda will help you leverage online business, clever marketing, and innovative digital technology to expand your reach, your impact AND your profits! She's a qualified coach and intuitive business guide which means she combines marketing savvy, technology know how and intuitive masterful coaching to serve clients globally.

Connect with the Author
www.RomanceYourTribe.com/belindajackson

Build your business with a sense of joy and celebration because it doesn't all have to be hard work.

Book Quotes *with Janet Beckers*
www.RomanceYourTribe.com

5 'Customer Love' Tips

People become your customer for THEIR reasons, not for yours. Here are five (5) compelling reasons, if you action them, why people will become, and more importantly, stay your customer (and love you more):

1. **People Want Convenience** – these days we're all 'time poor', so make sure your product or service gives them everything they need to get the outcome they want easily.

2. **People Want Results** - make it clear to your customer the RESULTS they'll get (or achieve). So don't just focus on the features and benefits of your 'product' or 'service' but also the results they'll get.

3. **It's Not About 'Information'** – people will become your customers if you take them on a Journey and not just give them a bunch of information.

4. **You Make the Unknown Known** – we don't know what we don't know. So give your prospects and customers everything they need so there's no 'missing pieces'.

5. **People Want Support and Encouragement** – so stay connected and supportive, add in your passion and personality and let them 'buy' the authentic and passionate You

And if you're ever in doubt what to do or give, ask yourself what you'd love to get as a customer - from you.

About the Author: Paul Godden

Paul Godden brings over 30 years working with video to a range of programs showing anybody how to tap into and use the power of video. Programs include 'Video Made Easy for Business', 'iVideo Mastery', 'Tube Video Domination', 'Animated Biz Videos' and other programs.

Connect with the Author

www.RomanceYourTribe.com/paulgodden

3 Tips To Start A Movement

🔲 🔲at i🔲🔲o🔲r 🔲 o🔲e🔲 ent🔲

Your movement is your BIG why. If you want to stand out and inspire people to like, trust, and fall in love with you, share your movement. People don't get obsessed with gadgets and services. They get obsessed with people and movements. Your movement is a snapshot of your values… and the reasons why you're so passionate about your work. It paints a picture of a better world.

How to get clear on your movement.

Tip #1 — Get clear on your personal values… the stuff that matters to you (example: freedom, lifestyle, integrity, happiness, harmony, etc.).

Tip #2 — What makes you happy? Write it down. You're looking for a list of things that make you happy (example: freedom, hanging out with my man or friends, feeling grateful, good coffee, travel, creativity, etc.).

Tip #3 — Write your movement.

My movement is: inspiring people to be FREE (free of limited thinking & free of fear)… so they can live happier & courageously create their (non-conformist) freedom lifestyle. I help people say, "YES!" to their dream life, (because freedom is… having choices + being able to do whatever you want)! Join me!

About the Author: Monika Mundell

Monika Mundell is the go-to Communication Strategist & Clarity Coach for women in business who want to liberate their time & accelerate their success with irresistible (fun) marketing. Monika helps clients infuse their brand with personality and presence, and profit with ease, with clear, captivating copy.

Connect with the Author

www.RomanceYourTribe.com/monikamundell

"Business Tribes want leaders to simplify, filter and inspire. You can do that."

Book Quotes with Janet Beckers
www.RomanceYourTribe.com

How to Show Your Clients Why You Are Meant To Be Together.

Standing out in a competitive market place is hard. As a health professional, it's tempting to try and be an all-rounder, and attract everyone you are qualified to treat. Instead of being everything to everyone, find your perfect clients and focus on what makes you their perfect match.

1.   **Get clear on the CLIENTS YOU LOVE**– As a Speech Pathologist, I'm qualified to work with many communication issues. But there is one particular type of client that makes my heart sing – helping people with disabilities learn to communicate, so they can achieve their full potential. Which of your clients make YOUR heart sing?

2.   **What makes you THEIR PERFECT MATCH?** - What makes you different from other people offering similar services to you? For me, it's the ability to help parents find the right tools for their child, and give them the support they need to use those tools to help their child communicate. WHAT'S YOURS?

3.   **What makes YOUR RELATIONSHIP UNIQUE** – There are plenty of great health professionals out there, but it's hard to know which one you should choose. I love creating Speechy TV episodes so people can get to know me before they decide to work with me. How can you SHOWCASE YOUR WORK so your perfect clients can get to know you?

About the Author: Gail Bennell

Gail is a Speech Pathologist who coaches parents of children with disabilities on Skype, so their kids can learn to communicate and reach their full potential. She also helps health professionals thriving build thriving private practices so they too can help their clients reach their full potential.

Connect with the Author
www.RomanceYourTribe.com/gailbennell

Video Love Messages

When someone visits your website you want to make them feel welcome and loved, plus quickly guide them to take action. Here's a script guide I use for my clients and you can use too.

- ✓ **Hey how's it going?** [Use your own words/style of expression for welcome greeting]
- ✓ **If you're watching this video it is probably because:** [Define them e.g. describe your ideal client and their current problems/issues that you can solve.]
- ✓ **Here's what I've got for you:** [Describe how you can help them with the problem/issue they have e.g. a way to get from pain to pleasure island.]
- ✓ **Here's what you can do to get it:** [Describe the Call To Action e.g. Add your email address in the box to receive the free webinar.]
- ✓ **Who the hell am I and why am I doing this?** [Finally share who you are and your mission]
- ✓ **Having worked with** [explain your experience and results in solving problems]
- ✓ **This offer is for:** [Reminder - Define them again e.g. describe your ideal client and their current problems/issues that you can solve]
- ✓ **Thanks for watching, I look forward to working with you**, [be sure to add your name / Call To Action. [Final Ending]

About the Author: Emily Miller

Emily Miller is a tech savvy, heart-centered Virtual Assistant and Online Media Goddess. Her clients are Rising Stars ready for the next level of success and visibility. She provides high vibration done for you services, removing your overwhelm, to create a conscious consistent online presence that delivers a profitable return.

Connect with the Author

www.RomanceYourTribe.com/emilymiller

Re-Program Your Self-Confidence

How you connect with your customers and the level of success you achieve depends a lot on where you are at personally. Psychologically, being an entrepreneur often challenges confidence levels due to business ups and downs. Most significantly however, it is important to focus on building your own confidence as your potential customers can sense if you don't believe in yourself, and then there will be a disconnect of trust in engaging with you and your business.

Here are three easy steps to higher self-confidence:

1. Reprogram your thinking with hypnotherapy audios. To help you I have created a free 'Confidence Building' hypnotherapy MP3 you can use. The link is below.
2. Create an evidence log of your own awesomeness.
3. Create a spreadsheet or journal of what little steps you have achieved. Remember, no major achievements occur without doing and acknowledging the little steps.

When you believe in yourself and have increased levels of confidence, customers will connect with you much more easily and be more ready to sign up to your programs. By empowering yourself, you empower your business and your clients.

About the Author: Kathryn Kitto

Kathryn Kitto is well experienced in the psychological ups and downs of business, with previously owning three different businesses. In her current psychotherapy and hypnotherapy clinic Healing Souls, she has created the Empowered to Shine Movement, which helps women to have the courage to go deeper to release their blocks to success and to have the confidence and self-belief to create empowered businesses.

Connect with the Author

www.RomanceYourTribe.com/kathrynkitto

Courting

Hey, you may have made it to the second date and your perfect client has joined your mailing list, but, just as in a romance, don't assume they are a sure thing. At this stage the relationship is still a bit one-sided. You are still doing the hard work to impress.

Here's some ideas to sweep them off their feet with your communication before you start making the sale.

Remember our Gift to you:
Online Tribal Business Leader Quick Start Kit

www.RomanceYourTribe.com/actiongift

Time Is Precious: Give Them Your Full Attention

Time is one of the most precious resources anyone has. Why? Because we have a finite amount of time available - once it's used it can _never_ be given back. In our 24/7 world, it's easy to get caught up in life's busyness.

That's why I help entrepreneurial minded clients to get strategic on managing their precious time, energy and focus – so they can use it wisely! Anyone spending time with you invests this precious resource with you. Show you value it by giving your full attention.

1. **Put away your gadgets.** It's amazing how often people _don't_ do this. Instead they talk and interact with their gadgets at the same time.
2. **Clear your mind.** Empty your mind of its busyness before discussions. Spend a few minutes sitting quietly with focused breathing or meditation.
3. **Choose your environment.** Have your meeting in a location or space which frees you to be focused and present.

Focusing your attention encourages a safe space, reduces tension and builds trust. It also supports hearing spoken, unspoken, subtext and subtle messages about what's going on for them. Focusing your attention saves time and helps people feel special.

About the Author: Lisa McDonald

Lisa has 11+ years' experience coaching people to strategically manage their life, unlock more potential, achieve more goals and live a healthy inspired life. Her holistic approach combines goal setting, personal growth, income creation, business and natural therapies. Lisa's integrated approach educates, inspires and empowers clients to transform their life.

Connect with the Author

www.RomanceYourTribe.com/lisamcdonald

Tips for Live Global Summits

Organizing a global summit, (interviewing guest experts on live Google Hangouts) requires a lot of preparation and teamwork to get it done right. The effort is well worth the results of creating huge visibility and going from being virtually unknown to superstar status fast online. One client doubled her list in 3 weeks and built a consistent residual income from monthly affiliate commissions from people who signed up to her / speaker's programs/services that now covers her living costs. She also grew an awesome community and developed some great business opportunities.

Preparation for successful google hangouts:

- Plug in your Ethernet cable and switch off WIFI
- Use a headphone set with a good microphone.
- Add lower third to display host's/speaker's name.
- Breathe. Remember FEAR is just EXCITEMENT without the breath.
- Set your intention for the interview.
- Do some power poses and listen to some high vibe music.
- Remember that you are EQUAL to your guest and that they are probably nervous too!
- Step into your role as HOST of this summit. As the person who pulled this whole thing together.
- Visualize the interview being fun, informative and amazingly well received by your audience.

About the Author: Emily Miller

Emily Miller is a tech savvy, heart-centered Virtual Assistant and Online Media Goddess. Her clients are Rising Stars ready for the next level of success and visibility. She provides high vibration done for you services, removing your overwhelm, to create a conscious consistent online presence that delivers a profitable return.

Connect with the Author

www.RomanceYourTribe.com/emilymiller

Romance Your Customers:
if you try to go for the hard sell too quick, you'll leave them feeling like a one-night-stand!

Book Quotes *with Janet Beckers*
www.RomanceYourTribe.com

Making a Connection

How many times have you received a call or called someone and you know they really are not listening? Okay they have their own agenda. However if you want to make a connection, you must allow the person to talk and you must actively listen too. When a potential client contacts me, I make sure that I address all their questions.

Making a connection is key. What is your potential client is looking for? Yes, many times I think they are trying to figure out want they want. Of course, it is important to see if you are a right fit for them and vice versa. So what can you do to connect with them?

Listen, ask what their vision is, relate on the same level, build trust, and don't be pushy. Of course, I also direct them back to my website to sign up for a free eBook.

About the Author: Nancy Barnes

Nancy Barnes is a Board Certified Holistic Health Practitioner and Certified Bodywork Therapist. She is Founder of College of Holistic Health, which offers tutored home-study holistic health programs. Nancy is also an Amazon Best Selling Author, Co-Authoring How Life Coaching Changes Lives.

Connect with the Author

www.RomanceYourTribe.com/nancybarnes

Meet Your Tribe

I was recently thinking about how to "meet" my potential customers when most of them live interstate and overseas. Building relationships is a bit easier in person when I can say "hello", shake their hand, establish eye contact and let them see who I am, in person. Online it's different - I got to "meet" Janet online through her weekly videos and realised that I felt that I "knew" her even though we've never met face-face.

So ... the answer is "videos" as a way of meeting people, establishing trust and developing relationships. YouTube is a perfect way to start; it is easy to use, is free, most people already know it and you can now have "business" channels connected to your main one. Yes, it can feel daunting establishing an online video presence. But just like dating; you need to meet your customers and introducing yourself. So get your phone out, use the video to say hello, post it and you've done the hardest bit.

Remember; be real, provide valuable content, and respond to comments. As people get to know you, they are more likely to think of you when looking for the service you provide.

About The Author: Kay Ross

Kay's expertise in health, education, coaching and online business growth is the basis for her success. She developed "Nurse Wellness Project" and "Nurse Biz Solutions" to support nurse's health and wellness and business development. Kay used social media to reach over 6000 nurses to talk about their health and wellness.

Connect With the Author

www.RomanceYourTribe.com/kayross

Invite Your Customers to Events & Conferences

As an expert, you are probably exposed to all sorts of events, networking and training opportunities that your customers could benefit from. You can personally invite customers to events that you think they would benefit from or you can share event information via social media and email. If you see an event being promoted on Facebook, for example, it's easy to share the post on your Facebook page.

There might also be opportunities for you to offer discounts to events specifically for your customers. This really makes customers feel special. Everyone loves a discount and if you're the one to give it to them, all the better.

If you're at an event that a lot of your customers are attending, why not put a call out on social media to catch up on the breaks or go out for drinks or dinner after the event. Many people attend events by themselves and are more than happy to meet up with other people they know.

You may even like to hold your own training or network event just for your customers where they can learn a specific skill that you can teach or they can network with each other.

About the Author: Ayesha Hilton

Ayesha Hilton is an author, speaker, and business strategist. She helps business owners, consultants, coaches and entrepreneurs grow their business and brand by becoming a published author. She is passionate about helping people do what they love while earning a great income.

Connect With the Author

www.RomanceYourTribe.com/ayeshahilton

Remember to Nourish Their Souls

In business, we tend to focus the most attention on how our customers see us- websites, graphics, packaging, storefronts. But the irony is that the things that really make for a standout business, known for making a difference, are the things we do that the customer never sees. It's the love and passion we pour into a new product, the intention, generosity, and dedication that drive us to deliver the best product or service we can.

When we focus so intently on the deliverables of information and products, we run the risk of creating consumption fatigue in our customers. What if, instead, you gave your customers something thoughtful? Not as a marketing tool, but just to create more beauty – visually, experientially, emotionally – in the lives of your customers.

We think that what our customers need is more meaning in their lives. But what they really long for is nourishment for their aesthetic sensibilities. One **way** to do this is to include a thought-provoking, inspirational quote in your weekly newsletter. It's not a platitude. It's not business related. It's meant simply to inspire.

Find some ways you can create moments of aesthetic nourishment for your customers. It will set you apart.

About the Author: Paula Tarrant
Paula Tarrant is a mentor and intuitive guide for creative women who long to do the work that lives in their hearts while living the life they're meant for. Want to make a good life doing work that inspires you while living true to who you are? Begin your journey today.

Connect with the Author
www.RomanceYourTribe.com/paulatarrant

A Smile Says It All

A smile says it all. I know, it's a simple thing, but oh boy, it makes the difference to my energy and connection when teaching and working with my coaching clients. Won't you give it a try? Here's what to do - just before you're about to pick up that phone or log in to Skype - smile! Yep, really pull your lips and mouth into a great big fabulous toothy smile.

Now, you may not feel like it, but let me assure you, but the time your client is saying 'Hello??' you will almost be laughing out loud. So any tension or anxiety your client may be feeling starts to dissipate - 'cause you sound so darn happy and they're catching the energy of it now too. Put a note on your computer screen, screen saver or phone - SMILE! May you bring light and laughter to you, your clients and the world around you.

About the Author: Louise Brogan

Louise is a great advocate of the KISS principle - Keep It Simple and Smile! She also loves helping people live an Abundant life by teaching them foundational financial skills and introducing them to their Money Personality.

Connect with the Author

www.RomanceYourTribe.com/louisebrogan

How do you know if you are achieving your goals unless you are actually measuring to see if there are changes?

Book Quotes *with Janet Beckers*
www.RomanceYourTribe.com

Write A Card A Day...

After a debilitating bout of arthritis, I complained to a friend that I'd lost my verve for life.

"You need to take your eyes off yourself and put them on other people. Do something to make others feel good" he said.

His words were like a slap. There I was having a pity party and I forgot that the best way to get my drive back was to give back.

I remembered the clients who had supported me over my past 20 years of being a sharemarket Mentor through my website – www.tradinggame.com.au. Gratitude swept over me. For 12 months I chose a client per day, and wrote them a card. I poured love into every word I wrote. I aimed to fill up my precious supporter's hearts, and to show them how much I appreciated them.

The care I received back from my darling clients wrapped around my soul like a warm blanket. I reclaimed my 'va-voom' for life.

I encourage you to show your heart to your tribe. Open up. Let them in. Rain appreciation onto them. Allow your light to shine, and ... I guarantee, your supporters will give back to you 100 fold.

About The Author: Louise Bedford

Louise Bedford is one of Australia's most compelling sharemarket speakers and she has trained thousands of people to maximise their own trading potential. She has degrees in Psychology and Business and is a best-selling author. You owe it to yourself to find out more about Louise's Mentor Program Course.

Connect With the Author

www.RomanceYourTribe.com/louisebedford

The Art of a Great Listener

If there is one skill that I believe that has propelled me to success faster than any of my other skills or qualifications is the ability to really listen.

I utilise 3 steps to engage in actively listening:.

Seek out Information: Let your client speak, don't interrupt them. Let them tell you their story, their pain, their challenges, their anguish and heartache. It is amazing what information you will receive by allowing them to pour their heart out. My first consultation is always in an investigative manner. The client feels validated, and heard, often for the first time in their lives. You are creating the space that allows them to feel worthy of being heard.

Talk less than you listen: When it is your turn to talk, it is essential that you are askingask questions to open up the client rather than you giving your advice. This is done at a later stage. Look for non verbal queues; they can be powerful indicators of what is not being said.

Actively Listening: This is essential to not just be waiting to speak, working out what you are going to say. Maintain eye contact, turn off your phone and put it away, remove distractions, nod and position your body to be facing the client in a relaxed manner.

About The Author: Lisa Tassell
I've been fortunate enough to work with many people to unlock their true potential and my own. I have over 14 years of experience in natural healing. I have combined my training as a Naturopath and my Intuitive Counselling with the blending of quality essential oils. Through this specialised approach profound, yet gentle transformations occur.

Connect With the Author
www.RomanceYourTribe.com/lisatassell

Answer Questions Before They Are Asked

Create a simple email series - which aims at welcoming, educating, and supporting your new clients. In many cases your clients/customers will have unspoken questions or concerns following a purchase - and this is completely normal. These questions are GOLD. For every question you receive, you can be certain there are others having similar thoughts and experiences. By addressing these before you are even asked, your clients will get a sense that you really get them.

This works on so many levels.

- Your clients feel supported AFTER the sale.
- They get useful information.
- The information they have now makes SENSE, because they now have your product/service to interact with.
- And it reassures them that they have made the right decision by choosing you - reducing issues such as chargebacks, "buyers remorse" or a totally preventable gradual disillusionment.

This is a strategy I not only use myself, but teach my clients to use - as it is one of the easier 'techie' things which I can teach them to do. It helps my clients gain the respect of their customers, and is often their first introduction to a practical online marketing skill. It's a win-win-win.

About the Author: Urszula Richards

Urszula Richards helps small businesses have a website presence they can understand AND control. By adopting 'the path of least resistance' approach, she teaches her clients only what they need to know right now to get them to the next step on their overall online journey.

Connect with the Author

www.RomanceYourTribe.com/urszularichards

Love In The Time of Video

These days if you're a businessperson, Love is something that you want to be showing your customers. The most powerful way you can show that Love (besides face-to-face) is through the medium of video.

Here's a Few Tips to Get you Started:

- ✓ These days all you need is a smartphone, some apps and a few simple accessories to make great videos.
- ✓ You can get started now by getting clear on who your 'ideal' customer is, the message you want to convey to them and what you want them to do.
- ✓ Once recorded, you upload to YouTube (a free video hosting service) and then share the link to the video with your customers.
- ✓ Put a photo of your favourite customer or a loved one near or behind your camera and simply talk one on one with the person in that photo.

Today's business currency is "Knowing, Liking and Trusting" the person you're doing business with. So if you believe your business provides a valuable service then you owe it to them to connect and share. So go on, show the Love to your prospects and customers in the best possible way.

About the Author: Paul Godden

Paul Godden brings over 30 years working with video to a range of programs showing anybody how to tap into and use the power of video. Programs include 'Video Made Easy for Business', 'iVideo Mastery', 'Tube Video Domination', 'Animated Biz Videos' and other programs.

Connect with the Author

www.RomanceYourTribe.com/paulgodden

Tune In To Your Client

One of the challenges I face as a designer is ascertaining a client's personal taste and style. Like everyone else, your life's experiences will have 'coloured' your feelings for particular colours. And your type of personality will attract you to certain pattern shapes and styles of decorating.

Being able to 'tune in' to my clients' relationship to the various colours and into their personality allows me to deliver a unique and personal design solution to each of them. It saves me loads of time when selecting fabrics, wallpapers etc and also builds great rapport. My clients often say to me 'You must be able to read my mind or else we share the same taste.'

I have developed a process to discover their colour preferences, including the tones of colours that resonate with them. There are a series of questions with visual cues that also allows me to determine their design and style preferences.

From the answers, I am able to define their 'colour personality'. I can then choose colours, fabrics and furnishings that I know they will love. And it is easy for me to choose a colour scheme that I am confident will bring them joy.

About the Author: Judith Briggs
Judith Briggs is a colour designer and author. She inspires her clients to bring the joy of colour into their homes and lives. Judith believes our home is our reward for a hard day's work. Coming home to one that resonates with us is nothing less than we deserve.

Connect with the Author
www.RomanceYourTribe.com/judithbriggs

Can Your Email Subscribers Feel The Love?

Potential clients value their privacy. Their email address is considered to be as sacred or as high value to them as their phone number. So, it can be difficult to build your email list without giving them a gift in exchange for their generosity. This gift can be an MP3 file, an article, a short video, or even an e-book! It has to be of high quality and high value, though. No fluff! If you come across as willing to offer valuable information for free whenever possible (instead of just a pushy sales person), then it increases your credibility in their eyes. You are trustworthy. This will help you to generate sales without asking for it.

In your automation email, say a little about yourself, and engage your prospect into a conversation with you. I ask my email subscribers, "What are you struggling with today?" to prompt a response from them. This is important: ALWAYS respond to each email that you receive with a response from this question. Be genuine. It is the start of your relationship with them, and it can make or break your rapport. Be engaging, but take it slow; it will lower their guard towards you.

About the Author: Belinda Bowler
Belinda Bowler, also known as Lindy Lopez, is the founder of Lindy's Life Coaching. As a spiritual light worker and intuitive consultant, she truly enjoys helping others when she can. She provides unique, empowering life coaching sessions with a precognitive advantage to passionate people seeking massive results in their lives.

Connect with the Author
www.RomanceYourTribe.com/belindabowler

Reframe your emotions: 'I'm not overwhelmed, I am calm but also, at the same time, excited by the possibility of what I am doing'.

Book Quotes *with Janet Beckers*
www.RomanceYourTribe.com

How To Rev Up The Romance And Become "Sexy" To Your Tribe!

Yes, yes, yes. I'm all for romancing your audience—starting off the relationship with a gift you know they'll love (your freebie opt-in offer) and then nurturing that relationship with your pearls of wisdom (your newsletter and videos).

But when you REALLY want to attract attention—all eyes on you, following your every move!—take a trip somewhere you love, doing business while you're on the road, and document your travels for your audience.

Travel stories powerfully connect you with your audience. They follow your journey and live vicariously through you. They lean in, pay closer attention to everything you say.

Tell your travel stories in your newsletters, and see your readership grow (and get more responsive). Tell travel stories in your marketing copy to capture attention and increase sales. Tell travel stories in your videos, and make a lasting impression. Tell travel stories on stage to fire up your audience.

But it's not JUST the stories that make you "sexy" to your audience. Feeling more alive while you travel gives you an inner glow that magnetizes and inspires your community as you share your stories.

So go on. Get your "sexy" on. Take a trip. It's good for business!

About the Author: Linda Claire Puig
Linda is an internationally recognized marketing expert who helps solo-business owners develop a portable, profitable business they can take with them anywhere in the world. She's the founder of the Portable Profits Club and Swap My Office, a global home-exchange community for entrepreneurs who love to travel.

Connect with the Author
www.RomanceYourTribe.com/lindaclairepuig

Take the Time to Talk

Talk to people, show them you are interested in them and listen to them.

Share your story when the time is right. This is where you get to know a little more about the person who has been drawn to you (for whatever reason).

You are in a powerful place of influence.

I talk to people who visit my café - everyone has a story. Everyone wants to be listened to. Everyone is looking for an answer. Yes they may not always want the solution or answer that you are providing ... just yet ... but they are on your doorstep. They may not buy from you right now but there is a whole lifetime in front of you ... and you are the one they have been drawn to.

You can do this in blogs, chatrooms, social media groups according to the investment of time and energy you make in reaching out. Communicate by giving helpful and relevant information on topics being talked about in these groups. You can also do this with newsletters, webinars/teleseminars, webTV.

When speaking to people live you can only access a relatively few people. By doing it on-line the world becomes very small.

About the Author: Cheryl Ueding

Cheryl Ueding (Australia) is the Owner and Founder of Soul Star Connections® and Producer of SoulStarConnectionswebTV... Shifting Gears in Your Life. She has developed spiritual self-development programs and home study courses: Shifting Gears®, Living Authentically, Be Your Own Healer... Be Your Own Life Coach; the Emotional Rescue® healing process and Facilitator Training of these. Co-author of Embraced by the Divine book.

Connect with the Author

www.RomanceYourTribe.com/cherylueding

Romance

If you've swept your client off their feet by courting them then they will now be "into" you. The relationship is going both ways and that's what you want to encourage. Here's some ideas to give you strategies to encourage your clients to interact with you and your brand.

Remember our Gift to you:
Online Tribal Business Leader Quick Start Kit

www.RomanceYourTribe.com/actiongift

Involve Your Customers in Decisions

Asking for someone's opinion is a great way to show you respect their ideas and value their input.

If you are creating a new course, writing a book or coming up with a new product - put it out there to your clients for their input on names. Having been involved in its creation and the decision process they will feel a natural affinity to the product, and feel an important part of your business.

Facebook is a great way to hold quizzes and start up conversations or group chats. Everyone loves to put their 2 cents in, and everyone loves being told their idea is a good one. Your interaction with all the input (making sure you thank and praise everyone for their efforts) and even offering a small prize for the best suggestion will really get the ideas flowing. Don't forget to announce the winner! Since the ideas have been suggested by your clients, they will obviously be words that resonate with your target market and potential clients.

I get clients to name the new smoothie recipes I create and serve them each month - it's one less job I have to do!

About the Author: Clancy Lee Beck
Clancy Lee Beck is the go-to personal trainer and weight loss coach for the over 40's who want to be Fit, Fabulous and Frisky.

From dynamic classes, to private strategy sessions and online courses, she helps clients achieve their lifestyle and body transformation goals.

Connect with the Author
www.RomanceYourTribe.com/clancyleebeck

Create Loyal Customers & Reward Their Loyalty

Your loyal customers are your biggest asset. They are the ones that become raving fans and advocates for your business. They have the biggest impact on your bottom line. They are more likely to respond to your marketing and promotions. They are the ones who will buy your products or services more frequently and tell all their friends how great your business is.

You want to create and maintain as many loyal fans as possible. The best way to do this is to reward them. Implement a loyalty program where you offer enticing rewards to say thank you. You could reward customers for liking Facebook page, following you on Twitter, referring a friend, signing up for your newsletter, entering a contest, or submitting a review.

What you offer as a reward may depend on what action they have taken and what type of business you have. For example, in your customer has purchased an introductory product, you could offer a discount on a more expensive product. Or you could offer then a discount coupon they can apply to future purchases. A reward might be a simple as acknowledging them on social media for liking your page or becoming a follower.

About the Author: Ayesha Hilton
Ayesha Hilton is an author, speaker, and business strategist. She helps business owners, consultants, coaches and entrepreneurs grow their business and brand by becoming a published author. She is passionate about helping people do what they love while earning a great income.

Connect With the Author
www.RomanceYourTribe.com/ayeshahilton

You set your intentions each day when you write your to-do list. Why not take control and set Emotional Intentions as well?

Book Quotes *with Janet Beckers*
www.RomanceYourTribe.com

Become the Meeting Place

Provide forums where people can engage and interact socially with a specific purpose. These can be instigated by you or by them.

At our café we have people who meet regularly with a set group of friends and others who use the space to have their office meetings. We have created a safe space where private groups of people with common interests can feel a part of and they then spread the word and gather others.

We also provide the opportunity for people to attend lectures, workshops and sessions with myself and/or joint venture partners. I particularly like to be able to offer the space to those people who have been very loyal to me to use to promote their own businesses.

You can do this on-line with specially-focussed forum groups and create community/global projects or challenges which the group may be showing an interest in or passion for. Any way that provides interaction with a specific focus on achieving something - particularly for the greater good - but staying true to your bigger vision. This is where you really get to become involved with each other (your target market) and you become more intimate with each other.

About the Author: Cheryl Ueding

Cheryl Ueding (Australia) is the Owner and Founder of Soul Star Connections® and Producer of SoulStarConnectionswebTV… Shifting Gears in Your Life. She has developed spiritual self-development programs and home study courses: Shifting Gears®, Living Authentically, Be Your Own Healer… Be Your Own Life Coach; the Emotional Rescue® healing process and Facilitator Training of these. Co-author of Embraced by the Divine book.

Connect with the Author

www.RomanceYourTribe.com/cherylueding

Spotlight Your Customers

One of the things I am most passionate about in business is making it easy for people to take action. When they do, I celebrate by shining the light on them and sharing their successes (large and small) with the world.

I do this in a few ways:

1. Member Spotlights on our Facebook Page
2. Rising Stars Radio: a podcast devoted to interviewing the action takers in our community
3. Email promotions
4. Dedicated webinars with members who have really kicked some goals.

As well as genuine excitement there is a strategy to spotlighting your customers. If you shine the light on others you get to bask in the reflected glow. It's a win-win-win really.

1. **Your customers win:** because you are shining the light on them and celebrating their achievements.
2. **Your potential customers win:** By seeing case studies of the people you work with they get to decide if you and they are a perfect match, before they become a customer and join your tribe.
3. **You win:** The customers you spotlight become extra loyal to you, other people get to see the results you achieve with your clients, and new customers are already pre-sold before they see your offers.

About the Author: Janet Beckers

Multi-award winning entrepreneur, Janet Beckers transforms entrepreneurs with a message to share into Tribal Business Leaders Online. Janet specialises in helping authors, coaches, speakers and small business owners step up, step out and get their message out to the world with her signature RYT training programs.

Connect with the Author

www.RomanceYourTribe.com/janetbeckers

Express Your Love

Words of Affirmation. That's just one of "The Five Love Languages" according to a book by Gary D. Chapman. I love his idea of saying all the things you love about someone; in this case, expressing this love to a client … a perfect client.

Do you know what makes a client perfect for you?

Perfect is not a character judgment; it simply means that what they need and what you do are aligned. They're a perfect fit for your gifts and talents, and also a joy to work with.

I affirm for all my clients what makes them a perfect fit for my brand. I told Robyn Chuter, a Naturopathic Doctor in Australia:

"Robyn, I love working with you. Your work to help your clients heal from disease makes a huge difference in the world. You have a BIG vision for yourself. And best of all, you implement!"

Affirming clients makes them feel seen and appreciated. When they meet others who might benefit from working with you, it's clearer to them who would be a good referral.

When you affirm clients, you re-affirm for yourself your priority, making it clearer in your mind, your behaviours and your results.

About the Author: Samantha Hartley
Samantha Hartley of Enlightened Marketing helps coaches, experts and entrepreneurs create Jaw-dropping Client-getting Messages™ so they attract perfect clients, increase prices 30-800% and become more joyful business owners.

To find out how to get more potential perfect clients to say, "OMG, I need your card!" visit http:www.EnlightenedMarketing.com

Connect with the Author
www.RomanceYourTribe.com/samanthahartley

Connect With What Really Matters

Help clients, friends and family to feel special by taking time to identify their core values, and applying that knowledge. There's loads of benefits! Remember goals based on core values provide strong foundations for building personal and business success. That's why I take entrepreneurial minded clients, who want to achieve more goals, through a step by step Values Identification process. It tunes them into their heart, rather than what they think they should want.

Benefits to them: Their core values are driving hot buttons. They're the secret to helping them to feel connected, inspired, empowered, successful and fulfilled. Reviewing values encourages strategic management of time, energy and money. It increases their ability to thrive.

Benefits to you: Learning and applying values demonstrates individualised attention. It supports specific communication, facilitating relevant examples and language. Conversation flows more quickly, easily and effectively. It conveys their importance and demonstrates your desire for them to thrive. Lacking clarity increases conflict, uncertainty and indecision. It also reduces focus, motivation and energy.

Make them feel special - connect them to what really matters:
1.   Their most important values
2.   How they love to spend their time, energy and money
3.   How their goals support them their values

About the Author: Lisa McDonald

Lisa has 11+ years' experience coaching people to strategically manage their life, unlock more potential, achieve more goals and live a healthy inspired life. Her holistic approach combines goal setting, personal growth, income creation, business and natural therapies. Lisa's integrated approach educates, inspires and empowers clients to transform their life.

Connect with the Author
www.RomanceYourTribe.com/lisamcdonald

"People are no longer content to be at arms-length with a business and brand. They expect to be able to interact with individuals, with real people, and to build a relationship."

- *Quick quote from page 8*

Book Quotes
with Janet Beckers
www.RomanceYourTribe.com

Create a Welcoming Hub

Create a welcoming environment that invites your customer to show up, relax, bring their friends and return to.

I do this by providing a coffee and antique shop. I wanted a "people place" where people could just come and experience the beauty and energy of a loving place filled with beautiful things and where they could access books on spirituality and healing. The coffee and food needed to match and we made it predominantly gluten-free because of food sensitivities. We provide a "quiet reading room" where books can be accessed.

I had no other intention than the cafe be aligned with my ideals and my long-term vision of creating a nurturing and healing space for people. The spin-off has been that my target market and alliance partners have naturally been drawn to me. They get to see my work and join my mailing list by subscribing to Soul Star Connections webTV.

You could provide a similar "hub" by creating a website/private chat/facebook group where kindred spirits would feel a part of and who would bring others.

You could provide ideas, challenges and swap stories to generate the "welcoming and cared for" attitude that we provide in the coffee shop.

About the Author: Cheryl Ueding

Cheryl Ueding (Australia) is the Owner and Founder of Soul Star Connections® and Producer of SoulStarConnectionswebTV... Shifting Gears in Your Life. She has developed spiritual self-development programs and home study courses: Shifting Gears®, Living Authentically, Be Your Own Healer... Be Your Own Life Coach; the Emotional Rescue® healing process and Facilitator Training of these. Co-author of Embraced by the Divine book.

Connect with the Author

www.RomanceYourTribe.com/cherylueding

You attract a tribe online by clearly articulating what you stand for in your market place.

Book Quotes with Janet Beckers
www.RomanceYourTribe.com

Romance Your Tribe With Photos

I run lots of events. I have groups of mainly women, with numbers of anything from 10 to 150 participants.

I also love to capture the moments and emotions so take lots of photos.

After the event I create a small photo slideshow video to music from them and post it to Facebook. My tribe absolutely adores them and repeatedly play it.

It reminds my tribe of the amazing time and transformation that was had. If I use a song at the event I make that my song in the video so that it can anchor them back to the event anytime.

This also makes them feel part of a community and I feel everyone loves looking over the photos. Putting them to music in a fun way is even sexier. It also creates interest for others who may like to attend your next event.

Here are the steps:

1. Remember to actually take the photos (ideally nominate someone in the group to do this)
2. Create the video/slideshow. There are free online programs to do this or use your computer.
3. Share the link all over social media.

Watch all the comments as your tribe feels romanced.

About the Author: Luanne Simmons

I help women around the globe get their lives and businesses on purpose through embodying Pleasure, Power and Prosperity. I do this by identifying the #1 thing holding them back and help them turn it into their biggest strength, so they can express their feminine essence and enjoy a juicy, abundant life.

Connect with the Author

www.RomanceYourTribe.com/luannesimmons

Publish Collaborative Books with Customers

The book you are reading is my fifth book in collaboration with my customers. It allows me to fulfil one of my core business values, which is creating opportunities for people to take action to grow their businesses online. It also attracts new customers, retains customer loyalty, builds my mailing list as well as those of my customers and also creates a real buzz around my brand.

Here are a few tips I have learnt over the past 5 projects:

1. Choose a book topic that will attract readers who are your ideal customer
2. Make sure the topic is general enough your customers can all contribute something of value (for example, in my book "The Power of 100", women from around the world shared stories on how they stay focused on their dreams).
3. Keep the word count short and be very strict in enforcing it
4. Remind people they don't need to be perfect. You'll give them feedback
5. Insist all authors spread the word on the launch dates
6. List build: direct all marketing to a page on your website to capture email addresses
7. Invite VIP authors who agree to promote
8. Have fun. You're creating something new.

About the Author: Janet Beckers

Multi-award winning entrepreneur, Janet Beckers transforms entrepreneurs with a message to share into Tribal Business Leaders Online. Janet specialises in helping authors, coaches, speakers and small business owners step up, step out and get their message out to the world with her signature RYT training programs.

Connect with the Author

www.RomanceYourTribe.com/janetbeckers

Commitment

You and your ideal client know you are a perfect fit now. It's time to commit, make the sale and keep your customer for life. Here are some ideas to help you wow your customer after the sale and keep them loyal to you forever.

Remember our Gift to you:
Online Tribal Business Leader Quick Start Kit

www.RomanceYourTribe.com/actiongift

Surprise Your Client with a Gift or Card

When people sign up for my FAST Writing Bootcamp, I send them a special present and a card to welcome them on board. In my sales page, I don't mention this. I let it be a surprise when they get it in their mail box.

If you run online programs, it's a lovely way to bring the human touch to the digital exchange you have with customers and you will stand out against your competitors as so few businesses will take the time and effort to do this.

You can send a handwritten card or use a card and gift service. The type of gift you send will depend on your business. I like to send something relevant such as a funky memory stick for my clients so they can save a back-up of their book.

Set up a system for sending out cards and gifts to make it easy for you to manage. Don't forget to include the cost of the card and gift in the budget for your program delivery.

Bonus Tip: Record clients' birth dates so that you can send them a card wishing them a happy birthday. You customers will feel very special!

About the Author: Ayesha Hilton
Ayesha Hilton is an author, speaker, and business strategist. She helps business owners, consultants, coaches and entrepreneurs grow their business and brand by becoming a published author. She is passionate about helping people do what they love while earning a great income.

Connect With the Author
www.RomanceYourTribe.com/ayeshahilton

Attitude of Gratitude

When business is not going as well as you'd like, it's easy to focus on the lack of income or new clients, because that is the problem you are observing each day.

A simple change of focus however can dramatically improve your mindset, and your business.

Gratitude is a magical thing. Showing your gratitude to existing clients with a free gift or service works wonders - it makes people feel special.

By appreciating the clients you have, your energy and focus will shift from one of lack, to one of abundance, making you a whole lot more attractive to work with, and your clients will rave about you!

Earlier this year I decided to do something special for my clients. During the first week of each month clients now I get a freshly made smoothie after their exercise session.

They love it! We have excited conversation after each session, they are inspired to create their own healthy smoothies at home for their partners and children, and my sales of health food products increased. Plus they are talking about and looking forward to next month's 'Smoothie Week'. And the kicker was getting two new high paying clients the next week, without even trying!

About the Author: Clancy Lee Beck

Clancy Lee Beck is the go-to personal trainer and weight loss coach for the over 40's who want to be Fit, Fabulous and Frisky.

From dynamic classes, to private strategy sessions and online courses, she helps clients achieve their lifestyle and body transformation goals.

Connect with the Author

www.RomanceYourTribe.com/clancyleebeck

If you can clearly stand up and say "this is the idea our tribe believes in and here's the place online we can all hang out" you will naturally stand-out as a Tribal Leader online.

Book Quotes with Janet Beckers
www.RomanceYourTribe.com

Provide More Than They Expect

Whenever I launch a new product or guide one of my clients with their launch, I always give them more than they were expecting. This is really valuable for the relationship and trust that we wish to establish and build.

As you grow your own business, you naturally begin to build resource lists, procedures and templates that continue to save you time and energy and you soon realise how useful they can be to your clients and customers.

For example, with each and every product I launch, I provide extra training resources and bonus materials that complement and enhance the learning process. For each of my clients, they are generally provided with guided templates, unlimited free email access to ask questions or submit ideas, resources such as graphics, audio/video stock and much more.

When you know what works in your own business, you know what will work for your clients and customers (after all, you've already discovered you are compatible). It costs nothing more than the original investment to provide these resources to your client. What your client gets in return can be a 1000% return on investment or more! No wonder they want to keep coming back to you!

About the Author: Karen Thomson

An Online Marketing Consultant since 2007, Karen trialled and tested several launch processes against the standard 'big bang/scarcity' methods of marketing gurus. What resulted was increased sales; especially for women in business. Karen now teaches the various techniques she discovered through products, programs and personal coaching via her website.

Connect with the Author

www.RomanceYourTribe.com/karenthomson

Keep In Touch Like Friends

The amount of commitment you put into your business and clients will determine the amount of customer appeal. Myself, I work to establish and have long-term commitments with all my clients, a few dating back from the beginning of my business in 1997. I get to know and go-the-extra-mile for each client as if I only work for that client. I strive to have my clients feel like they can get a hold of me at any time and that they know where I am and what I am doing.

My clients are my friends. I keep in touch throughout the year:

First, in January I send out a personalized letter and if a tax client, a tax organizer.

In May, I send out a post-tax season survey; and a special on a mid-year financial review.

At the end of August I send out a special to all my clients for a "Before it's Too Late" tax planning review.

In October, I recognize my VIP clients as my Boss and send them a Bosses Day card.

Then in December I send a Holiday card and coupon. All this allows me to keep in touch throughout the year with all my Very Important clients!

About the Author: Cynde Canepa
Cynde Canepa has provided Administrative & Financial Assistance to guide businesses to financial safety since 1997. She specializes in Business / QuickBooks Consulting & Trainings. She is Enrolled to Practice before the IRS and licensed to perform Business & Estate/Trust Tax Preparation and Planning.

Connect with the Author
www.RomanceYourTribe.com/cyndecanepa

Thoughtful Gifts Don't Need to be Expensive

To show my clients appreciation, I give them a little gift here and there. Who doesn't love a surprise? Sending a gift to my clients is a fun way for me to show them that I care and that I have a commitment to them. And as the founder of The College of Holistic Health it also reinforces my message to my clients to take time out for themselves. Most importantly it says I appreciate them.

The gifts do not have to be expensive or even cost a dime. For example, I found beautiful colorful reusable shopping bags for a bargain. Now my clients get one with their course materials. Other gift ideas are: an inspirational book, herbal tea, eye mask, bookmark, meditation CD, eBook, or a card.

You can send a gift anytime. It could be a scheduled time, or when you are inspired to, when someone needs a pick-me-up, or a special time of the year. I love finding treasures as much as giving them, and besides I love shopping. However, bottom line is that commitment to my clients is the most important part of my business.

About the Author: Nancy Barnes

Nancy Barnes is a Board Certified Holistic Health Practitioner and Certified Bodywork Therapist. She is Founder of College of Holistic Health, which offers tutored home-study holistic health programs. Nancy is also an Amazon Best Selling Author, Co-Authoring How Life Coaching Changes Lives.

Connect with the Author

www.RomanceYourTribe.com/nancybarnes

Make Their Journey Easier

Based in a rural area, my clients often find it hard to get good quality health products and supplements at an affordable price. To get the products I suggest means they either have to drive a considerable distance, spend hours searching the internet, pay for postage or pay hefty small town prices.

Sourcing quality products for your clients that help them towards achieving their goal, or enhancing their journey with you, can make you invaluable to them, and provides an additional service they may not be able to get with a competitor.

Source the products at wholesale prices, then on-sell to your clients at just below retail price. Combine several clients' orders together and postage is negligible for each client. You both win. You make a profit on the sale and they make a saving. Plus you get a very happy client who feels you've done them a favour, and are looking after them. They get quality products at a discount, and you make their journey with you easier.

Having a delivery of items awaiting them adds excitement to their next session - everyone likes to receive a box of goodies!

About the Author: Clancy Lee Beck
Clancy Lee Beck is the go-to personal trainer and weight loss coach for the over 40's who want to be Fit, Fabulous and Frisky.

From dynamic classes, to private strategy sessions and online courses, she helps clients achieve their lifestyle and body transformation goals.

Connect with the Author
www.RomanceYourTribe.com/clancyleebeck

Create Special Memories through Unique Actions of Appreciation

It's amazing how often entrepreneurs will spend their time searching out new customers and clients rather than taking great care of those who are already doing business with them.
For lower end clients something as simple as a surprise eBook, teleseminar or report can go a long way to create customer loyalty. Often, those who invest just a little will turn into higher end clients when they feel appreciated and cared for.

What about your high end clients? When's the last time you surprised them with a "for no other reason than I appreciate you" gift that is delivered by courier or mail.

Not long ago, one of my private clients hosted her first-ever live event. To let her know how proud I was of her accomplishment and willingness to stretch, I had a bouquet of flowers delivered to the location of her event to arrive just as she was beginning the event. She was unbelievably surprised and incredibly appreciative that I did this.

You may be surprised at how much loyalty you create by taking care of the customers and clients you already have rather than continually prospecting for new business at the risk of losing what you already have.

About the Author: Kathleen Gage
Kathleen Gage is the "no-nonsense, common sense" online marketing strategist, speaker, author, product creation specialist, and owner of Power Up For Profits. She helps entrepreneurs make money online. Her clients are driven by making a difference through their own unique voice.

Connect with the Author
www.RomanceYourTribe.com/kathleengage

In business you are judged on the results you get, not on how much you know. You can only get results by taking action.

Book Quotes *with Janet Beckers*
www.RomanceYourTribe.com

The More You Give the More You Get.

As entrepreneurs, we know that to do our business well, we must be passionate about it. It is equally important to convey that passion to our customers, especially loyal customers. Just because we "have" the client doesn't mean they will stay with us forever. Assuming you have a fantastic guaranteed product or service, your customer still needs to feel the love from you regularly.

As soon as you have a new customer, say thank you! Do it via email or an old fashioned handwritten note or even a Starbucks gift card saying thanks for keeping my business brewing!

Remember an annual event each year. On my "Rodanniversary" (the year I joined my company), I send a note to all of my customers and thank them for their loyalty and their impact on my life. On my birthday, I give away a gift to one lucky customer whose name I have drawn. If you are a representative of a company, like I am, make sure you help them with their selections. Reach out to them monthly, before the company does...they are your customer, the company just happens to supply the product.

The more we give, the more we get, in referrals and continued customer loyalty!

About the Author: Lauren Mescon

Lauren Gordon Mescon, attorney and former family court judge, was introduced to the entrepreneurial world of Rodan + Fields and direct sales by a lifelong friend. She was immediately hooked and today has a successful business which she can work from anywhere with only a laptop and nearby coffee shop!

Connect with the Author

www.RomanceYourTribe.com/laurenmescon

Make Customer Service Your Passion

Customer retention is a top priority. I run a wellness lifestyle coaching company with a variety of programs and packages. I include my customers' service needs as one of the most important values of my company vision. Excellence in customer service is my passion. There are a number of ways to deliver a top customer-oriented service.

1. Listen to your customers
I stay in touch. I ask customers specific questions about their experiences. I send a short survey to my list to ask if they feel they are getting valuable content or programs. If I get less than positive comments, I follow up personally by email to ask what I could do better.

2. Be innovative
I want my customers to have the very best programs I can offer. I constantly attend trade show events, network with my peers, take tele-trainings, in an effort to keep up with the latest trends.

3. Keep up with the competition
I watch what competitors are doing, seeing if there are new ways to deliver services that others don't provide. It's important to differentiate myself from the competition, so that my customers get cutting-edge services.

About the Author: Carol Davies
Carol Davies is a certified success coach, speaker and author with Passion Motivator Coaching. She helps busy women and entrepreneurs who are overwhelmed in personal and/or business life find their passion, get focused, devise a life plan and achieve success with joy and ease.

Connect with the Author
www.RomanceYourTribe.com/caroldavies

How to Make Your Customers Feel Loved With a Phone Call!

When somebody makes a purchase, I follow up and make sure that they actually got what they ordered. This serves three purposes. First, it avoids creating frustrated customers who possibly didn't get what they ordered, it helps to solidify their trust in the relationship, and it shows that you're paying attention and that you care.

I also like to call customers periodically and check in with them between purchases. They are usually surprised and delighted to hear from me and they truly appreciate it. They don't expect to hear from me personally, and the fact that it is me and not someone in my office, or on my team, means a lot to people.

Talking to my customers personally helps me improve my business and it helps me understand what they need better so I can give them more of what they want. And finally, it keeps me on their radar so that the next time they need something they come to me, which can lead to affiliates commissions, referrals, and more business.

Going the extra mile and connecting with your customers creates loyal customers and bigger profits and is well worth the effort!

About the Author: Ellen Violette

Ellen Violette helps independent professionals, entrepreneurs, small businesses, and authors gain instant credibility and expert status with digital publishing and #1 Best-Seller KDP launches, along with building high-income businesses for her clients. She is a regular contributor to Published! Magazine, a #1 best-selling author, and a Grammy-nominated songwriter.

Connect with the Author

www.RomanceYourTribe.com/ellenviolette

Just like a beautiful long-lasting relationship, the first person you need to learn to love and understand in your business is yourself!

Book Quotes *with Janet Beckers*
www.RomanceYourTribe.com

Use Video in Twitter for Customer Service

Are you using your Twitter company account to stay in touch with your customers and give them information of value? This is a great way to provide outstanding company service in a unique way. Many of your customers have profiles on one of the social media platforms, especially Twitter. They are eager to know better ways of doing business to streamline their processes or how to do business better. Why shouldn't they use some of your company's products or services to accomplish this aim?

Make a short video explaining how one of your services can help improve their business process to reduce their costs. For example, if you have an accounting service, highlight useful but little-known business tax tips the customer can easily implement with your company to help them save money. Put these tips in a brief video showing a Power Point presentation. Upload it to YouTube or directly on your website homepage. Then send the video link to your customers' Twitter account.

Customers love free information on how to improve their business profits. Video is one of the top ways to connect with them. Do this to provide great customer service.

About the Author: Carol Davies
Carol Davies is a certified success coach, speaker and author with Passion Motivator Coaching. She helps busy women and entrepreneurs who are overwhelmed in personal and/or business life find their passion, get focused, devise a life plan and achieve success with joy and ease.

Connect with the Author
www.RomanceYourTribe.com/caroldavies

Bonus Chapter

I hope you have enjoyed the ideas shared with you by our authors and more importantly, I hope you are inspired to take action and implement a different tip each week this year.

We are grateful for any feedback you care to give and the best way to do that is to share your thoughts on Amazon, Kindle, Social Media or simply email us at theteam@wonderfulwebwomen.com and tell us what you think.

As a thankyou, I have a bonus chapter for you from the book that inspired our community to join together and share action tips for you to implement, *"Romance Your Tribe Online: The 5 (and a half) Steps To Create a Tribe of Loyal Fans Who LOVE Your Brand".*

You can find out more about the book and the growing number of "Action" books in the Romance Your Tribe Online Series over here at www.RomanceYourTribe.com.

Love, Janet Beckers

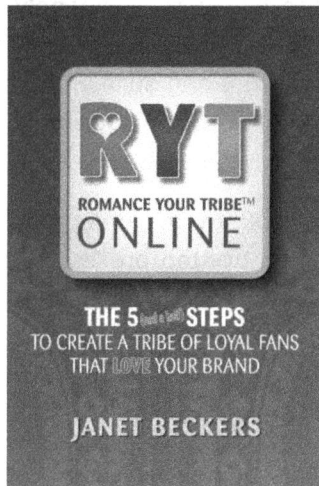

Tribes and Romance

I know you can do this. I know you can attract to you a tribe of loyal fans online who LOVE your brand.

Why do I know this? Because now, more than ever before, individual entrepreneurs and small businesses have an advantage over big business. The playing field has more than levelled.

You see, the rapid explosion in social media has changed the way we do business online. People are no longer content to be at arms-length with a business and brand. They expect to be able to interact with individuals, with real people, and to build a relationship. This is challenging for big businesses to do. It is simple for a small business, if they have strong brand foundations in place.

There are huge opportunities for entrepreneurs to establish themselves as Tribal Leaders. A leader who creates a place for a tribe to focus online and ideas and common language that connect them. The exciting thing is, these leaders are not only limited to the charismatic communicator we normally associate with leading. If you can tap into your unique story and style and create products and services that are branded with your unique language you have the building blocks to naturally rise as a Tribal Leader.

That is the purpose of this book. By the time you finish the last chapter you will have the step-by-step process to tap into your unique profitability, intimately understand your most profitable customers, have packaged your expertise into trade-markable programs and set up a Tribal Platform online that attracts, nurtures and sells to your ideal clients on auto-pilot.

I know you can do this because you now have a process to help you. A process that works. Let me outline it for you below.

Tribes Online

We have entered the Tribal Age of The Internet.

Until now, focusing on solving the needs of your customers has been enough to build a strong foundation for your business. But that's changed, thanks to the internet. Now your customers and potential customers actively interact with each other online. They expect to interact with you and your brand as part of a community or tribe.

It started a few years ago with blogs, where people could leave comments and have their "say," rather than just passively reading something like a newspaper. The popularity of forums skyrocketed, and people were having deep, active, and enduring conversations online.

Then along came Facebook, Google+, Twitter, YouTube, LinkedIn... the last few years have seen an EXPLOSION of ways people interact on the net. The old ways of doing business on the internet have been swept away by this interactive revolution. This is because...

We all share a fundamental human need to belong.

We all hunger to find a group, community, or tribe to interact with – this happens at a lightning pace on the internet. People are making buying decisions based on peer recommendation and what they hear via social networks.

Do you like what they're saying about YOU or your business? Do you even KNOW what they're saying about you or your business?

If you don't think it's important, just listen to a few of these facts...

• 78% of consumers trust peer recommendations

• Only 14% trust advertisements

• YouTube is the 2nd largest search engine in the world

• Facebook has taken over Google as the most popular web site

• 25% of search results for the World's Top 20 largest brands are links to user-generated content

• Social Media has overtaken porn as the #1 activity on the Web

It's literally a different world than it was just a few years ago...

We're now in the Tribal Age of the Internet. This is the new "Connection Economy", and it's the people who know how to tap into these tribes that'll survive and thrive in online business.

What Is a Tribe?

Seth Godin, the author of many best-selling books, including "Tribes: We Need You to Lead Us" defines tribes well: *"A tribe is a group of people connected to one another, connected to a leader, and connected to an idea. For millions of years, human beings have been part of one tribe or another. A group needs only two things to be a tribe: a shared interest and a way to communicate."*

Tribal Leadership

As you can see, from what I've shared above, people definitely have a way to communicate. The other two elements needed for a tribe, according to Seth, are a leader and an idea. This is where you come in. There is a huge opportunity for people to step up and lead and, with an overwhelming number of communication distractions, people are hungry for someone to do just that. Tribes want leaders to simplify, filter and inspire. You can do that.

If you can clearly stand up and say "this is the idea our tribe believes in and here's the place online we can all hang out" you will naturally stand-out as a Tribal Leader online. If the "idea" is core to your business message, then you will create a tribe of fans who LOVE your brand.

The exciting part is Tribal Leaders are no longer limited to those rare charismatic people we normally think of as leaders. The nature of the internet and the way it brings millions of people throughout the world together, means there are endless opportunities for "ordinary" people (not that there is anything remotely ordinary about you!) to attract a tribe by clearly articulating what you stand for in your market place. The tribes that can develop around your brand, not only share your passion but are also loyal and profitable.

The 5 (and a half) Steps to Romance Your Tribe

Over the years I've been fortunate to interview hundreds of the most successful people in online business. I've explored with them what has made their businesses so successful and how they have created tribes of loyal fans. Even though each person was very different, and their businesses unique, there were clear patterns and a system emerged.

I have since gone on to introduce this system into my own business (with wonderful results) and mentored hundreds of clients to implement this system over incredibly diverse industries. Simply put, it works.

I'll be guiding you through this system in this book. Let me introduce you to each step here so you have a big picture view of the process before we dive into the detail.

Step 1: The Profit in You

Just like a beautiful long-lasting relationship, the first person you need to learn to love and understand is yourself!

In chapter 3, I share a very personal story with you of transformation, both business and personal. I then teach you the 9 step process to create massive change in your life and the 3 mindset approaches you need to embrace so you are ready to step up as a Tribal Leader.

In chapter 5, we dive in and uncover your unique knowledge and story that is the foundation of your tribe. The definition of tribes I shared earlier states that tribes form around an idea. We'll look at your ideas in this chapter.

At the end of this step you will have identified the unique story and expertise that no-one else can replicate. The core that is the foundation of your profitability.

Step 2: Your Profitable Avatar

When you're searching for the "perfect one" for your long-term relationship, you will have your "wish list" of the perfect man or woman. You know what you want, and you'll know them when you meet. The same holds true for your business.

Your Profitable Avatar represents your ideal customer. Not just the one who likes what you do and wants your products and services. We're talking about the one who'll commit to that long term relationship and happily pay!

We'll get very clear on this person in Chapter 6 when I introduce you to the simple, and very powerful, Profitable Avatar Quadrant Exercise.

At the end of this step you will know exactly who your most profitable potential customers are and how to easily identify and attract them.

Step 3: Your Signature System

When you're looking for romance, how do you present yourself so your idea soul mate understands just how incredible you are? It's about communicating and paying attention to how you present yourself (what you see is what you get baby)!

When you have implemented the first 2 steps in The Romance your Tribe System you will have already laid a strong foundation to be the trusted advisor many customers in your industry will choose. They will identify you as someone they resonate with, who understands how they think, and can act as their trusted guide.

In chapter 7, we set you apart from everyone else in your industry with your unique branding language and system. We then create product and service packages which leverage your expertise and maximise your profits.

At the end of this step you will have a trade-markable signature system that sets you apart from everyone else in your industry.

Step 4: Joint Venture Mastery

So you're clear on who your ideal soul mate is, you know you have something wonderful to offer them and you know, when you meet them, you'll be able to dazzle them with the true you. So how are you going to meet them?

Where is Cupid when you need him?

In romance, Cupid may be your well-meaning friend who keeps setting you up with blind dates. If you aren't clear with your friend about what your perfect date is, and you're not talking to a friend who has your ideal date in their social circle, then you're going to have a lot of bad dates!

Cupid, in business, is a Joint Venture partner. In chapter 8, I'll guide you through the process to identify Cupid for your business. We'll look at the common mistakes people make when approaching a JV partner and what to do instead. I'll share the simple formula I use (and my clients have used with consistent success) when sending an invitation to a potential JV partner and the method I used to launch my business that put me on the International business map in a matter of 8 short weeks.

At the end of this step you will know exactly how to identify and approach ideal joint venture partners and have systems to work with them to dramatically increase your profitability.

Step 5: Romance Your Tribe

The process of finding potential new clients and moving through the process of becoming a paying customer, in fact a raving fan, is very much like a romance. If you try to go for the hard sell too quick, you'll leave them feeling like a one-night-stand! If you treat every new lead in your business as if they are going to be "The One' you will spend the rest of your (business) life with, then **you will see how the Romance Your Tribe model works to build a business of customers committed to you for life!**

In this step I'll walk you through the 5 stages of this "romance" and how it ties together all the things you need to put in place to have an automated online business. You'll see how all the moving pieces fit together. I refer to this as your Tribal Platform.

Step 5, actually has 5 sections and each is covered in their own chapter. Here is an over view.

Flirting

Flirting is the stage most people think about when it comes to marketing your business online. This is the traffic generation part. The part of the business building cycle where you put on your sexiest clothes, paint on the lippy, put on the push-up bra, scan the headlines so you'll have something to talk about and head out to find your soul mate (men, you can skip the lippy and push-up bra OK). The business building equivalent is finding great sources of your ideal customer and making such a great impression on them they can't wait to get back to your place.

In chapter 10, we'll revisit the Profitable Avatar Quadrant Exercise you did in chapter 6 and use it to strategically target your marketing to attract the ideal client who will actually pay you and be great to work with. I'll then share the 3 most effective flirting strategies that get you the best results and are the favoured strategies of the hundreds of my colleagues I have interviewed too.

At the end of this step you will know exactly how to find and attract new leads to your business who are most likely to spend money with you and consistently bring new traffic to your website.

Back to My Place

Now you've been out flirting around you should have lots and lots of gorgeous potential customers excited to get to know you better. It's time to invite them back to your place. Like in a romance, you want to make sure, when you invite them home, that the place is looking the best it can. In romance, this would mean cleaning up, strategically placing your trophy collection somewhere they will notice, putting on some mood music, candles and generally making them feel so comfortable and welcome they agree to a second date.

In business (and list building specifically), this means ensuring your web site is designed to convert visitors you attract to become subscribers on your list.

In chapter 11, I'll share what you need on your website, the best software to use, how to make your website irresistible to your Profitable Avatar and then we'll cover some advanced techniques to increase conversion and also credibility.

At the end of this step you'll now the most important things to include on your website so you convert visitors to subscribers and build a mailing list of people who love what you do.

Courting

The courting phase is where you're really keeping in touch with them. They're ready for another date with you, and you're serious about developing a lasting relationship with them. In online terms, after they've signed up for your e-mail list, you'll follow up with your newsletter and your e-mail auto-responders.

You may have made it to the second date but, just as in a romance, don't assume they are a sure thing. At this stage the relationship is still a bit one-sided. You are still doing the hard work to impress.

In chapter 12, I share how to automate your courting and the best strategies that are working right now for you to consistently build a long term relationship with your new subscribers. We'll cover strategies from email sequences to podcasting to online TV. Then I'll detail 3 great strategies you can use to court that create income at the same time as they create a stronger relationship.

At the end of this step you'll know how to communicate with your new leads to turn them into raving fans. You'll know the best strategies using writing, video and audio and know how to automate everything so you don't have to work so hard.

Romance

This is where they're starting to give you a little attention now – they're starting to get "into" you. The relationship is going both ways and that's what you want to encourage.

In chapter 13, I share a few different strategies you can implement in your business to create true loyalty and romance with your tribe.

I outline strategies to encourage interaction and then cover in detail 2 specific strategies of collaborative projects and competitions. I'll also introduce you to my unique 4th Win Test that will revolutionise the way you look at your marketing.

At the end of this step you will know very simple but powerful strategies that create true loyalty from your subscribers and make you stand out in your industry as a true leader. Even if you are totally new to business.

Commitment

This is where you're looking forward to a long-term relationship – and in romantic terms, this would be where you might start thinking about children. In business, this is where they become your customer, where they purchase your products – a very big step! They may start with your less-expensive products – a perfectly reasonable way to start! – and they'll go on to become a loyal customer who'll spend more and more money over time... and become a devoted, dedicated fan.

In the 4th step, when you created your Signature System, you determined the product packages you could offer. In Chapter 14, we get into the nitty gritty of putting it all together so you can create products fast and sell and deliver your programs on auto-pilot.

I cover how to sell a product with integrity of it hasn't been created yet and then the fastest way to create an information product based on your expertise (or that of others). I then detail 9 different business models you can use online and who they suit.

At the end of this step at the end of this step you'll know the best online business model for you and be ready to multiply your income while freeing up your time with automation and packaging of your expertise.

Step 5 (and a half): Surround yourself With a Support Network

So why do I call this the 5th and a half step? That's because, even though you can build a fantastic Tribal Platform and a passionate tribe online by implementing the first 5 steps, it is the magic half step that really allows you to step up and step out in a meaningful and sustainable way.

To really shine, every successful business owner knows they cannot do everything themselves. Even if they work from home on their own (which is what I do and what many of the successful business people I have interviewed do) they take responsibility for creating their own support team. They don't do this passively.

They actively create support in the following 3 areas:

1. Create a team of people who love doing what you find tedious.
2. Invest in a mentor
3. Create a Peer Mastermind Group

In chapter 15, I show you how to recruit and work with a virtual team, how to select a mentor and how to find and run a mastermind group. I'll also share my 7 step process to get your partner to support your dreams.

At the end of this step you'll know how to build a team to run much of your business and free you up to do more of what you love.

So, let's get stuck into it. I can't wait to share the Romance Your Tribe (RYT) system with you and hear of the results you get.

www.ingramcontent.com/pod-product-compliance
Lightning Source LLC
Chambersburg PA
CBHW060620200326
41521CB00007B/831